is for
Golden
years

Terri L. Glimcher

&

Tammy J. Mackey

G is for Golden Years
A Life Enrichment Guide for Senior Living
Senior Activities for Life Enrichment

First Printing: 2010

ISBN#: 978-0-557-97887-8

Originator and author: Terri L. Glimcher
Writer and contributing author: Tammy J. Mackey
Contributing Editor: Barbara Ellis
Cover & Interior Book Design: Studio 6 Sense • www.studio6sense.com

DEDICATION

We would like to start by thanking our grandparents for the positive impact they have made on our lives. Without their love and support, we wouldn't have an appreciation for the elders in our world.

We would also like to thank our children and grandchildren for the loving support they have offered through this endeavor. Thanks to the Mackey, Ellis, Smith, Phillips, Glimcher, and Burton families for their encouragement to complete this book.

Thank you to Barbara Ellis for your editing support and thanks to John Mongold for your ongoing friendship.

Lastly, we must thank the seniors who are, and have been making a difference in our lives on a daily basis. You remind us that life, like wine, takes on a particular quality as one ages. Our experiences, memories and interactions are what make us who we are.

Thank you for teaching us to be better people today and tomorrow, and to carry our torches into our golden years with dignity and grace.

CONTENTS

FAMILY RESOURCES

INTRODUCTION

Introducing Terri Glimcher

*T*erri is the Life Enrichment Director for a large senior living corporation located in Florida. She is the recipient of the 2009 Assisted Living Federation of America Senior Champion Award. The Orlando Sentinel has recognized Terri numerous times for her outstanding programming both with seniors and the surrounding community. She was a contributing writer for "Inside Elder Care" and has consulted and trained activity directors all over the country. Her life enrichment program is the number one choice for local high school seniors when completing their required internship hours. *USA Today* has featured her programs in their publications.

Due to the nationwide success of the Bridging The Generations program, a documentary was created by two reporters in Syracuse, New York.

Read the following blog statements from various people who are familiar with Terri's program:

"As a former secondary teacher, I can only wish that my school had been in your geographical area. What a great way to engender respect, engage intellect, and realize that we are all a part of living history. I look forward to your future articles

and I will definitely pass this one on to some of my old teaching compatriots!"

"Kudos to Terri! I was lucky enough to visit the facility where Terri is Activity Director. The minute she walks in the door, the faces of the residents light up. I spent hours talking to them, and all call Terri part of their family, not staff. I truly believe she has given these residents a gift, the gift of feeling alive, not just existing."

"Terri, thank you for all the work and time you devoted to pull Mom, Domenica, out of the shell the stroke put her in. The quality of her life was greatly enhanced by your efforts. I'm not sure if your "people skills" were natural or learned, but whichever, you're certainly on top of your calling."

"Terri, the passion you show for your job and your seniors is remarkable. I would definitely consider activities such as yours before I selected an assisted living facility for my loved ones. It appears that most facilities don't see activities as important for their residents. I think it is extremely important. Keep up the good work!"

Comments from the residents that participate in these programs:

"Thank you so much for the senior prom. My date was so handsome. I never got to go to the prom because we were so poor. Thank you, thank you for giving me the chance to have my senior prom before I die. I am so happy!"

"I love everything and all the activities. I wake up early and wait for Terri. I don't want to miss anything!"

"We have the best activities program and the best activities director. If you are bored it is your own fault. There is always so much to do!"

"I was so upset when my children moved me into assisted living. After a week here I started going to all the activities. Now I am having such a great time! I love the mystery lunches. I can't wait to get my name on the list!"

"I never thought I'd see the beach again. Then Terri took us on the bus to New Smyrna beach. I took my walker and went right down to the water. I took my shoes off and actually went in! It was delightful! Then we went to Daytona Beach on the water for lunch. I never thought I'd have that experience again in my lifetime. Thank you."

"I love bowling. I am 100 years old and I can't believe we are still going to the bowling alley! I used to bowl every week with my husband. It brings back great memories!"

"Cooking class is so great. We made my meatball recipe that I used to make for my family. It was delicious and everyone enjoyed it. I can't believe I remembered all the ingredients. Thank you Chef Tammy!"

"I had such a fun time at the Hoe Down. I danced the whole night with those kids! I could even keep up with them. I had so many dance partners; I couldn't even count them all. I won the dance contest you know!"

"I loved the mystery tour to the Crispy Crème factory. I never knew how they made a donut!"

"I laughed so much at the pajama party. Truth or dare was so funny! I never laughed so hard. Thank you for having that. I got to wear my new pajamas. The food was great too!"

The following are experiences that have transpired while interacting with the seniors.

I was in the activities room at 8 a.m. preparing for my day. As I'm working, I look up and along comes Gladys with no shoes, no hearing aids, and no teeth. Her hair was disheveled. "What are you doing?", I said. Gladys looked at me and simply replied, "What's going on now? I don't want to miss anything."

I once had an evening Pajama Party. It was posted around the lobby and elevator: "Come to the lobby at 6:30 in your favorite pajamas. Parlor games and fun." Lo and behold, as we were gathering in the lobby, one of my female residents came strolling in wearing a short, short, baby doll neglige. She stated casually as my eyes were popping out my head and my jaw was hitting the floor, "You said to come in what I sleep in, and this is what I sleep in."

In cooking class, we had all the ingredients for a dessert and a main dish. We told the residents the dessert was to be layered. Although the fruit and whipped cream were on the table, so too were the main dish ingredients. After some direction giving and moving about the group, I looked over to see the final product created by one of the groups. I distinguished layers of cake, blueberries, cheese, salsa, strawberries and mayonnaise as the topping. It was too late to say anything, so I didn't. The residents went ahead and ate it then claimed that it was delicious. Sometimes it's better to keep quiet.

We went on a dinner excursion to a favorite local chain restaurant. All appeared to be going well until I went into the restroom and left the group unsupervised for a few minutes. When I came back, I noticed the staff changing light bulbs. While I was gone, the residents had asked that the lights be changed to a higher wattage. Amazingly enough, the staff accommodated them and did it!

The prom is always a delightful event. High school seniors and the retirement community seniors get together for a prom. Sometimes the residents forget their age. When one female resident who is 98 met her date, who was 18, she just fell head over heels in love. She latched onto that boy and wouldn't let go. He was a good sport and treated her with the utmost respect. She later stated that if he had asked her, she would have married him.

One lady loves to dance. She loves it so much. When the music was playing and she had no one to dance with, she just pulled her walker out to the dance floor and used it as a dance partner.

One day two of our residents, husband and wife, put on some fancy clothes and went to the bank to withdraw some money. They attempted to withdraw millions of dollars. What they forgot is that they no longer even had an account with that bank. The teller was kind enough to offer them a danish and coffee and had them sit down and relax until we could arrive to take them back home.

The famous card game called "Uno" has taken on a new life here at our facility. No longer is the game called "Uno", but is now called, "You know".

An activity schedule is wonderful, however, the residents sometimes take things to extremes. If exercise class is supposed to start at 8:00 a.m. and at 8:01 it hasn't yet begun, they'll stand in the hall and start yelling. The Certified Nursing Assistants think there is an emergency and come running only to find the video has not been properly started.

"Oh my goodness. They gave me so much. I don't know how they expect me to eat all this." That's one of the favorite lines used by one of my folks. It never fails. I turn my back for a minute to have a conversation, and by the time I look again, all the food is gone and she's asking for dessert.

One story I've come to appreciate has been told to me by a 98 year old female resident. When she was a young woman, she was teaching in a one room school house. Two of her responsibilities besides teacher included fetching water, and collecting fire wood.

One of the gentlemen I work with told me that his job during the war was to decode Japanese messages. It's hard to imagine that he lived through those times.

It's funny how the folks I work with are limited when it comes to getting out of their wheelchairs if requested by the nursing staff. However, when the students show up to the dances, some of these same folks get up out of their wheelchairs, take off the oxygen and start dancing merely by holding the hand of those teens. The families are amazed at what their parents and grandparents can do when inspired.

In The Beginning

After a family has made the decision to move their loved one into your community, contact the family members either by phone or in person to introduce yourself. Begin to establish a relationship and assure the family that you will do everything you can to make sure their loved one is comfortable and cared for in her new environment.

Prior to arrival make sure the activity calendar is posted on the wall of the living quarters in large print within line of sight.

Make sure the resident's name is on his or her door when he or she arrives.

Leave a welcome basket with goodies and toiletries in the assigned apartment for the new resident.

Have a welcome committee of residents greet the new resident.

If there is a roommate, bring the new resident and the current resident together for a quiet, private introduction.

Meet the new resident and go over the calendar. Highlight the activities of interest to her and explain the incentive program.

Show the new resident her seat in the dining area and be sure she is aware of meal times.

Have the current resident give a tour to the new resident to show the building and where particular areas are located such as the nursing station, the hair salon, laundry facilities, and of course, the activities room.

Make sure the new resident is connected for mealtimes. Assign a current resident to go pick up the newcomer for each meal. They can then become more acquainted and will perhaps form a lasting friendship.

Introduce the new residents to all the department heads and address any concerns the individual may have.

Take the time to show the new resident the emergency escape routes and cover any other safety procedures.

Remember that new residents often feel their independence has been taken away. They give up their homes, their cars, and their spouses may have passed on. Life as they knew it, has changed dramatically. Have compassion and utilize good listening skills. Give the new resident time to adjust.

Chapter 2

Getting to know
your residents

When interviewing the new resident, provide a quiet private space for the resident to converse with you. Do not use a questionnaire when interviewing. It's impersonal. Just jot down a few notes and update them when you are in your office. Really talk and get to know this individual for who he or she is. Talk about interests and what she did before she came to the facility. Get a sense of where the person is cognitively, socially, and physically. Build trust.

Identify any adaptive equipment needs in order for the new resident to fully participate in the life enrichment program. Get him or her involved as quickly as possible. Uncover strengths and skills and set the person up to play a role in leading favored activities.

Once the new resident comes to activities, focus on creating relationships with other residents so she feels welcomed and comfortable.

If you don't already have one, set up a Guardian Angel Program. Pair the new resident with a staff member. The staff member meets five times with the resident and creates a personal relationship. The staff finds out more about the new resident and then shares the information with the other staff. This helps the staff get to know the resident better and the resident connects with the staff on a personal level upon entering the community.

Realize that you are one of the first people the new resident will bond with, therefore, he will often come to you with issues or concerns. Listen and assist where possible. Send along information to other staff that can address the individual's needs.

Call or email the family at least once a week in the beginning to let them know how their loved ones are transitioning. Be sure to get the family's email address so you can send them photos of their loved ones in action. Photos can communicate what words can't say. When the family sees something with their own eyes, it is likely to ease their concerns about their mother, father, or grandparent.

Chapter 3

Making it feel
like home

As the person in charge of activities, you are like a mini-mayor. Get to know your community members. Assist in setting up their apartments so they feel warm and welcoming. Have a gift basket filled with items of interest waiting for them when they arrive. Help them put up family photos, or help put together an album of fond memories.

Have them come to cooking class to make familiar recipes. Introduce them to the hair salon. Many people pride themselves in keeping up their looks. Hair and nail appointments are very important.

Try letter-writing sessions. If it's too frustrating to attempt to write, have a volunteer write a dictated letter. (Remember this information may be confidential and should be treated as such.)

Make a list of favorite TV shows with dates and times and post it in a conspicuous place in the apartment.

Chapter 4

Letting the residents know their lives make a difference

Seniors want to remain connected. They want to give back. Provide community service projects such as packing soldier bags, knitting blankets for the neo-natal unit, collecting school supplies for needy children, volunteering in the schools, stapling church bulletins, visiting others in the hospital, and collecting blankets for the animal shelter. Allow the seniors to participate in the programs that are near and dear to their hearts.

These projects afford the residents the fulfillment of knowing their lives are making a difference.

Chapter 5

Planning a healthy life enrichment activities program

*P*lan dignified activities. It is your job to include the experiences of the seniors of your community. Have an appreciation of their experiences and shape the program around the wants and needs of the seniors that make up your community. With honor and respect guiding your actions, a respectful program will ensue.

More is better. The more activities you plan, the more the residents will be involved. Once they go to their rooms, they are not likely to come back. Therefore, have a full activity calendar from morning to evening.

Plan for and include all residents regardless of their cognitive, physical, or social abilities. Make sure that you utilize adaptive equipment if necessary. For example, use large print cards for Bingo, or books on tape for people with limited vision. For an activity like bowling, use a ball ramp for someone that can't leave her chair. Use tables that will accommodate wheelchairs. Ask the occupational therapists for suggestions and use them as a resource when using unfamiliar adapative equipment.

One person cannot do it all. Utilize your surrounding community members to come in and lead activities. The following is a suggested list:

- Chefs from the local chain restaurants can lead cooking class.
- The local florist can lead flower arranging.
- The fruit stand owner can show how to make strawberry shortcake.
- Mary Kay cosmetics may be willing to do free manicures.
- The local pizzeria owner can allow the residents to make their own pizzas at his establishment.
- Local home health agencies can sponsor healthy snacks.
- College interns and high school students in need of volunteer hours can be used as a great addition to your program.
- Retired seniors from the community are always willing to assist.
- The Lions Club likes to celebrate monthly birthdays. They will often provide cake and small gifts.
- Professional bridge players can come in to teach and lead bridge.
- Poker players can do the same.
- Chess clubs can set up tournaments or individual playing partners.
- Crochet clubs can teach and set up projects.

- Realty companies are a surprising resource. Realtors like to establish relationships. Many homes are in foreclosure and household items may be donated to your program.
- Veteran groups will often honor veterans on patriotic holidays.
- Young adults with special needs are another great resource.
- Teachers from local schools can provide educational resources and student resources.
- Religious affiliations will often hold services or even come pick up residents to attend services. Members will often come in to lead a variety of activities.

Chapter 6

Creating your
Activities Calendar

Your activity calendar should contain activities that include emotional, cognitive, social, and physical aspects.

Socialization among residents is essential to a successful program. When the residents connect with each other, they want to make sure their friends are participating in activities with them.

The following is an example of a daily activity schedule:

8:00 a.m. Walking Club

Often there are sidewalks around the building that can be used as an exercise path or the hallways within the building can be used.

9:00 a.m. Group Exercise

Exercise with an activity leader or by video/DVD. Make sure people in wheelchairs can participate as well, "Exercise, Senior Style" is an excellent video.

10:00 a.m. Armchair Theater	
Take virtual tours all over the world through media. A snack from that country can be provided. This event can also be the basis of a follow up discussion about the country. This activity should take you through lunch. If not, plan an additional activity.	
1:00 p.m. Bingo, Trivia, Jeopardy, Brainteasers	
These activities are stimulating and engaging.	
2:00 p.m. Table Games	
Dominoes, "Uno", "Connect Four"	
3:00 p.m. Snack	
The residents can assist in preparing and serving snack.	
4:00 p.m. Word search, "Scrabble", jigsaw puzzles	
5:00 p.m. Dinner	
6:00 p.m. Nuts and News	
Serve peanuts (or substitute) and drinks and watch the news together.	
7:00 p.m. Poker, "Rummikube", Bridge	

Start the a.m. with one activity per hour, then after lunch, add additional activities. The most successful program has more than one activity going simultaneously. If only one activity is planned, those who do not enjoy that activity will go to their room to stay.

Often during the mornings, various congregations will hold services on property. Another option is to have the congregations pick up residents to take them to services.

Any activity that has food associated with it will bring in more people.

Special Note: Change can be very unsettling. Often you will see behavioral issues pop up if you introduce too many changes at one time. Do not make abrupt changes to the activity calendar once it has been running. Introduce new activities slowly.

Examples of Physical activities

Exercise class
> With a leader
> With a video/DVD

Walking
> Indoors
>> Hallways
>> Malls
> Outdoor
>> Sidewalks of the facility
>> Sidewalks of the community
>>> Check route for safety

Bowling
> Indoors
>> Set up your own modified lane
> Community Bowling
>> Call the lanes ahead of time and let them know your needs.

Dances
> Small group dances amongst the residents
> Large community dances with the outside community invited

Swimming
> Contact your local YMCA

Examples of Cognitive activities

Trivia
Use "Trivial Pursuit" or the Internet to collect questions

Bingo
Use large cards

Spelling Bee
Use easier words for those with less cognitive abilities. Don't keep score, just have fun. Have the residents use the words in a sentence.

Brain Teasers
Use the Internet as a resource

Remember When
Pick topics and have the residents share their experiences from their younger days

Name that Tune
Play music and allow them to guess the artist and the year

Wheel of Fortune
Set it up on a large white board and use a spinner for points

Connect Four
Purchase from the local department store.

Concentration/matching games
Purchase or create your own

Reading
Keep a well-supplied library. Get large print books. Use the community library as a resource.

Word search, crossword puzzles, "Suduko"
Purchase books, or print off the Internet

Solitaire
> Have large print playing cards available

Computer use
> Run simple computer classes and have a computer available for public use

Examples of Social Activities

Cooking
> Guest chefs
> In house cooking class
>> Be prepared

Crafts
> Try to create useful crafts, use volunteers whenever possible

High Tea Party
> Everyone wears a hat and tastes a variety of teas

Card games
> Bridge, Poker, Pinochle

Board games
> Have a variety available

Jigsaw Puzzles
> Have a table that can go undisturbed

Movies
> Movie night with popcorn

Watching sports
> Monday Night Football

Ice Cream Socials
> Create your own sundae or smoothies

Beading
> Some projects can be sold at the local flea markets

Pajama Party

Everyone comes in their pajamas and plays fun parlor games

Auction

Follow up from the incentive program

Dominoes

Have round table available

Gardening

Plant outdoors or indoors

Walking Club

Meet and go for a pleasant stroll

"Red Hats"

Set up your own or have a group come in

Gentlemen's club

Have the guys get together to discuss the good old days and watch sports together

Scavenger Hunts

Set up fun little hunts

Religious services

Set up a different service each day

Group Manicures

Have a volunteer come in to assist

Game Night

Group get-together to play a variety of games

Fondue Night

Get together with cheese or chocolate fodue

Happy Hour

Once per week with snacks, soft drinks, beer and wine, and entertainment

Entertainment from the community

This can occur during the day, or evening

Armchair theater
> Travel the world from a comfy chair through TV, videos, and DVD's

Music
> Sing-a-longs

What's in the Bag?
> Fun guessing game

Examples of Craft Ideas

No-sew fleece blanket

You will need sharp scissors, a yard stick or other measuring tool, masking tape, pins

Start with two complimentary pieces of fleece material that are exactly the same size. One piece with a pattern and one piece of a solid color works well.

Measurements that seem to work are:

- 2 pieces of 1 by 1 yard for a baby sized blanket
- 2 pieces of 2 by 2 yards for a child sized blanket
- 2 pieces of 3 by 3 yards for a twin sized blanket.

You can make larger blankets as you wish.

Remember that about 4 inches of each edge is going to be sliced all the way around to be tied together to hold the two pieces together.

Lay your two pieces of fleece out on a table. Flatten the blankets and make sure they are positioned edge to edge. Using straight pins or safety pins, neatly pin the material together about six inches in from the edges. This is to keep your blanket in place as you work. If necessary, trim all the way around to make sure that they match exactly and that they are perfectly square.

Now, at each corner, cut out a four by four inch square.

Once the corners are cut out, you are ready for the next step. Measure a straight line across four inches up from each edge meeting at the corners. Put a piece of masking tape from one side to the other. This will act as a stopping point when cutting strips along to edge.

Make cuts from the edge of the doubled fleece to the masking tape line. Each cut should be an inch apart. You can mark it ahead of time with chalk or a very light dot of a marker. Be sure to cut straight up. When you are finished with one side, you will have a fringe along each edge.

When you are finished cutting each side, start at one corner and begin to tie the fringe of the two layers together. Tie the same type of knot over and over for consistency. If more than one person is tying the knots, make sure they are all tying in the same manner. A square knot works; right over left, left over right and pull. Make sure the knots are snug. If you want to make it a little fancier, you can cut the edges of the fringe on a slight angle before tying.

Once you have tied all the way around, you can remove your pins. Pull gently all around to square out the blanket and you are finished.

You can go onto YouTube and put in "No-sew blanket" and you can watch a video to assist you.

Lollipop Plant

This craft makes a cute holiday craft. You can use a variety of lollipops including Blow Pops, Tootsie Pops, Dum Dums.

You will need:

- Small terracotta flower pots – 2-inch diameters or larger work well.
- Assorted acrylic paints
- Water base glaze
- Styrofoam - white or green
- Spanish moss

After gathering your supplies, come up with a theme and paint your pots. The following are some examples:

- St. Patrick's Day: green clovers
- Mothers Day: flowers
- Fathers Day: fish
- Valentine's Day: hearts
- Halloween: candy corn, pumpkins or ghosts
- Thanksgiving: leaves or acorns
- Christmas: trees, snowflakes or snowmen

Paint the clean, dry pot with acrylic paints. Let them dry completely.

After the pot has dried, apply water base glaze according to the jar instructions. Let the pot dry completely again.

Wedge a small piece of Styrofoam into the bottom of the pot. Push the lollipops into the Styrofoam, and then cover the foam generously with the Spanish moss.

Enjoy your decoration or give them away as gifts.

Examples of Trivia Questions

- **Mothers Day is on the third Sunday of May. True or False?** False, it's on the second Sunday in May

- **What is another name for Memorial Day?**
  Decoration Day

- **June 14th is Flag Day. How many stars are on the flag?** 50

- **Where was the Declaration of Independence signed?**
  Philadelphia, Pennsylvania

- **What is another name for Halloween night?**
  All Hallows Eve

- **Name three gifts that the Wise Men brought?**
  Gold, Frankincense, Myrrh.

- **What do you do when under the mistletoe?** Get a kiss.

- **What is the traditional flower of Christmas?**
  The Poinsettia

- **What song is associated with New Years?**
  Auld Lang Syne

- **What day is Martin Luther King Day on?** January 15

- **What colors are associated with Valentines Day?**
  Red, White, Pink.

- **Can You name the symbol associated with St. Patrick's Day?** Shamrock (three leaf clover)

- **What is another name for an Irish Walking Stick?**
  Shillelagh

- **Name the Sunday before Easter?** Palm Sunday

- **What is the Easter Flower?** The Lily

- **What are the astrological star signs and the two months that each sign represents?** (The symbols and precise dates are optional details and not necessarily required in quiz answers, especially since precise dates are open to debate.)

- Aries, the Ram - 20 Mar to 19 Apr (precise dates for all signs can vary according to interpretation)
- Taurus, the Bull - 20 Apr to 20 May
- Gemini, the Twins - 21 May to 20 Jun
- Cancer, the Crab - 21 Jun to 21 Jul
- Leo, the Lion - 22 Jul to 22 Aug
- Virgo, the Maiden - 23 Aug to 22 Sept
- Libra, the Scales - 23 Sept to 22 Oct
- Scorpio, the Scorpion - 23 Oct to 21 Nov
- Sagittarius, the Archer - 22 Nov to 21 Dec
- Capricorn, the Goat - 22 Dec to 19 Jan
- Aquarius, the Water-bearer - 20 Jan to 17 Feb
- Pisces, the Two Fishes - 18 Feb to 19 Mar

- **Who wrote: "Bring me my bow of burning gold: Bring me my arrows of desire..." ?** William Blake (1757-1827, English poet, painter and mystic.)

- **What famous slogan was originally devised by Patrick O'Keefe for the Society of American Florists?** "Say it with Flowers."

- **What connects the words sitcom, smog, brunch, muppet and cyborg?** They are all 'portmanteau' words, ie., combinations of two different words. (Sitcom is derived from situation and comedy; smog from smoke and fog; brunch from breakfast and lunch; muppet from marionette and puppet; cyborg from cybernetic and organism. The term portmanteau as description of word combinations was devised by Lewis Carroll when it first appeared in Carroll's book 'Through the Looking Glass, and What Alice Found

There', dated 1872, appeared in 1871. More about portmanteau words, and how to use them in creativity and development activities.)

- **What symbolic item did Lauren Bacall put into the urn containing Humphrey Bogart's ashes?** A whistle (the gold whistle was engraved with the words "If you need anything, just whistle" - reference to Bacall's lines spoken to Bogart in their first film together To Have And Have Not, released in 1944. Bacall was Bogart's fourth wife and they remained married until Bogart's death in 1957.)

- **Which one of these is on the coast: Cairo, Johannesburg, Tripoli, Sarajevo, Nairobi, Khartoum?** Tripoli (Libya)

- **Which one of these is not on the coast: Venice, San Diego, Reykjavik, Marrakesh, Helsinki, Lisbon?** Marrakesh (Morocco)

- **A famous leader's first name of Mohandas is commonly replaced by a first name that means 'great soul'; who was he?** Mahatma Gandhi (Mohandas Karamchand Gandhi, 1869-1948, Indian statesman and spiritual leader).

- **Who was the The Wizard of Menlo Park who said, "Genius is one percent inspiration, ninety-nine percent perspiration."?** Thomas Edison (1847-1931, US inventor of the light bulb, gramophone, electric valve, a megaphone, a storage battery, a system of electricity generation and distribution, and first person to produce talking motion pictures).

- **Paul McGann, Peter Davidson and William Hartnell have each played the same famous sci-fi role. What's the character's name?** 'The Doctor', or 'Doctor'.

(Not Dr Who. Dr Who is the name of the series. The character is called The Doctor).

- **What are these cities?** There is more than one answer for some (I've attempted to reflect the most common globally recognized associations; if you have local interpretations that you feel are more appropriate then that's fine - no need to let me know unless you feel especially strongly)
    - City of Dreaming Spires - Oxford, UK.
    - City of Magnificent Distances - Washington DC, USA.
    - City of the Angels - Los Angeles, USA.
    - City of Churches - Adelaide, Australia.
    - City of Love - Paris, France; Rome, Italy; Calcutta, India.
    - City of Peace and Justice - The Hague, The Netherlands.
    - City of the Tribes/the Eternal City/City of Love - Rome, Italy.
    - City of the Violated Treaty/Stab City - Limerick, Ireland.
    - City of the Violet Crown - Athens, Greece.
    - Crescent City - New Orleans, USA.
    - Empire City - New York, USA.
    - Fair City - Dublin, Ireland. (Also Perth, Scotland)
    - Forbidden City - Beijing and Lhasa, China.
    - Granite City - Aberdeen, Scotland.
    - The Harbour City/Emerald City - Sydney, Australia; (Wichita, USA is also known as Emerald City).
    - Monumental City/Charm City - Baltimore, USA.
    - Mormon City - Salt Lake City, USA.
    - Orchid City - Shah Alam, Malaysia.
    - Quaker City - Philadelphia, USA.

- Soul City - Harlem, New York, USA.
- The Stampede City - Calgary, Canada.
- Windy City - Chicago, USA.
- Motor City - Detroit, USA.
- Music City - Nashville, USA.
- The River City - Brisbane, Australia; Edmonton, Canada; Wanganui, NZ.
- The Steel City - Sheffield, England.
- The White City of the North - Helsinki, Finland.

Chapter 7

Outings

Make sure you have an emergency file on each resident. It must contain a recent photo, a list of medications, DNRs (**Do Not Resuscitate**) if they are applicable, insurance information and emergency contact numbers. Have water, a first aid kit, jumper cables and warm blankets available. Residents must be seat belted. Make sure the passenger vehicle is maintained regularly and is tested before loading the vehicle. Each person shall be assisted on and off the bus and all wheelchairs and walkers must be stored according to safety standards. All outings should be available to all residents whether ambulatory or in a wheelchair.

A great way to increase participation is to have a mystery lunch and tour. You set up the trip ahead of time, but the residents don't know where they are going until they arrive. Make sure the destination is somewhere they have never been. Also check it out yourself so you don't have any unpleasant surprises.

Dining Out

While some residents have the skill to order off a large menu, for others it can be overwhelming. Call ahead and ask the manager if he will present a limited choice menu. Also speak to the manager about your group and their needs. If you have a large number of walkers or wheel chairs, the restaurant staff should be informed.

The restaurant will usually set up tables ahead of time and assign wait staff that will be more patient with your group. Be aware that if your group includes folks with dementia, ordering and paying the bill can be very confusing. Have the wait staff write down the resident's names with their orders. This reduces asking questions like, "Who ordered the meatball hero?" Often times the folks have already forgotten what they ordered.

Be sure to call to thank the manager and send a note of personal thanks if the service was good. Calling the corporate office to give praise is another great way to appreciate the efforts of the restaurant and the wait staff.

Shopping

If you take your residents shopping, call ahead to make sure they have electric carts and that the store is not so large that it is overwhelming to the residents. Let the manager know when you have arrived and ask her to page you if the staff notices any issues with the residents. Remember too, the larger the space, the more scattered the seniors will be when they shop. This makes it more difficult to assist them if they need you.

Library

The public library is a great place to take the residents. Call ahead to the librarian and explain your needs. Ask that she meet you by the door to greet the residents and to give them a short tour and to explain the expectations for that particular library. Find out ahead of time what is needed to gain a library card and be prepared. At the end of the trip, the cards can be put into a folder to keep them safe and secure. Check the library schedule for activities you can attend. For example, our library has an opera once a month. The residents love it. Other special media presentations are also shown.

Chapter 8

Ways to
increase participation

---

*C*reate incentives. For every activity the residents attend they receive "funny money" in the amount of twenty. If they bring another resident with them to an activity they receive an extra twenty dollars.

At the end of the month, an auction is held. The auction items are new and interesting to the residents and have been donated by the merchants in the community. Approximately twenty dollars of the enrichment coordinator's budget is spent on this event. The items are based on interests voiced by the residents. The items included can vary from snacks to perfumes. Small appliances, jewelry, umbrellas and other useful items should be added. Many times the residents want items that are useful but are not going to clutter their apartments. Around the holidays specialty items can be placed out and purchased as gifts for family members. Sometimes this is the only opportunity that some folks have to buy gifts for their families.

It is imperative to keep statistics as to who attends the activities. If residents receive money for something they did not participate in or they get extra coupons from someone else, the entire economy of the system will collapse due to unfairness to the folks that did participate.

Job Fair

For people that may not be interested in actually participating in the activities, enlist their assistance to help run the activities. In this way, he or she can earn "funny money". Each person then has some choice as to how he or she wants to participate.

In talking to residents, one thing that is especially missed is the chance to be working and to be contributing to their community. One way to fulfill this need is to create jobs within the residential community. A list of internal jobs can be created such as taking statistics, watering the plants, leading classes, calling Bingo, passing out snacks, making snacks, happy hour set-up, setting up a general store, or knocking on doors and bringing other residents to activities.

The next step is to hold a job fair where the residents apply for the various positions. They fill out applications, reference sheets, and complete an interview with the activity director. They explain why they believe they are qualified for the position. This creates a great opportunity to get to know the person better and to pair them with a job that benefits them.

Once they are hired, they can earn $100 per week in funny money to shop at the general store that includes items like snacks and drinks.

Uninterested

If a resident does not come out of his or her room, sending another resident to make the invitation often works better than the staff going after the person. Have the "buddy" resident go to the door and personally invite the "hesitant" resident to come and sit with her for the scheduled activity. Be especially gracious and attentive to the "hesitant" resident to increase the likelihood of coming back to activities. Try to find out why she's not coming to activities and add in some preferred activities for that person. If a resident cannot be cajoled to come and participate, allow him or her privacy. Go back occasionally to re-invite but don't over do it.

Creative Titles

Sometimes when planning activities, the strategic use of different adjectives can entice the residents to want to sign up for the outings. For example, instead of "lunch out", call it "Mystery Lunch". A mystery lunch and tour can include shopping, a tour of Krispie Crème, a visit to Russell Stover's, going out to the movie theater, going out for ice cream, or going to the bakery outlets.

Instead of writing "exercise", call it "senior style exercise".

Instead of calling it a movie, call it "armchair theater".

Instead of calling it reminisce, call it "remember when".

When you post something like crafts, be specific as to what the craft is and make it sound inviting. "Spring is knocking and wants to be invited in. Join us in the art of flower arranging, led by Kim E, our local florist."

When you post cooking, post the recipe for the week. Ask the residents to submit a favorite recipe that can be used in cooking class. Utilize your local merchants as guest chefs.

Recipes

The following are a few examples of recipes that can be used with the seniors. Cooks.com is a good resource.

KEY LIME PIE

Printed from COOKS.COM

>   1-9" graham cracker pie shell
>   1-14 oz. can sweetened condensed milk
>   3 egg yolks (whites not used)
>   1/2 cup key west lime juice

Combine milk, egg yolks and lime juice. Blend until smooth. Pour filling into pie shell and bake at 350°F for 15 minutes.

Allow to stand 10 minutes before refrigerating. Just before serving, top with freshly whipped cream and garnish with lime slices.

EASY BANANA PUDDING

Printed from COOKS.COM

>   1 box instant vanilla pudding
>   1 sm. container whipped topping, softened
>   1 box vanilla wafers
>   3-5 bananas, thinly sliced

Make instant pudding according to package. When it has chilled, add the container of whipped topping to pudding.

Layer wafers, bananas, pudding. Continue layering until ingredients are gone. Last layer should be pudding.

CHICKEN CRESCENT ROLLS

Printed from COOKS.COM

> 2 c. chopped chicken
> 2 (3 oz.) pkg. cream cheese
> 1 tbsp. chopped chives
> 1 lg. bottle drained mushrooms
> 8 crescent rolls (unbaked tube)
> Melted butter
> 1 pkg. seasoned croutons, crushed

Mix chicken, cream cheese, chives and mushrooms. Unroll crescent rolls, fill with mixture and re-roll. Roll in melted butter and seasoned croutons. Bake in shallow pan 30 minutes at 375 degrees. Optional - top with cream sauce or chicken gravy.

---

7 LAYER BEAN DIP

Printed from COOKS.COM

> 2 cans bean dip (mild or hot)
> 2 cans guacamole
> 1 bundle of green onions, chopped
> 2 tomatoes, chopped (drained)
> 1 sm. can black olives
> 8 oz. pkg. cheddar cheese
> 1 c. sour cream
> 1 pkg. taco mix
> 1 extra lg. bag tortilla chips

First Step: Add sour cream and taco mix together and mix well.

Second Step: In a large platter dish, begin layering ingredients accordingly:

1st Layer - Bean dip
2nd Layer - Guacamole
3rd Layer - Sour cream
4th Layer - Green onions
5th Layer - Tomatoes
6th Layer - Black olives
7th Layer - Cheddar cheese

DIABETIC CHOCOLATE NUT BROWNIES

Printed from COOKS.COM

1/3 plus 1 tbsp. butter
Liquid sugar substitute to equal 1 c. sugar
3 tsp. vanilla
3 eggs, beaten
2 tbsp. cocoa
1 c. sifted flour
1/2 tsp. salt
1/2 tsp. baking powder
12 pecans, finely chopped

Combine butter, sugar substitute, eggs and vanilla. Sift together cocoa, flour, salt, and baking powder. Add liquid mixture and stir until well blended. Stir in nuts. Pour into a non stick 8 inch square pan. Level batter in pan and bake at 325 degrees for 20 minutes. Cool on a wire rack. Cut into 16 squares.

Chapter 9

Utilizing the community within

$\mathcal{M}$any of the residents have skills they can share. What's important to the residents is that they stay connected. By incorporating their skills within the activity schedule, it allows people to contribute to their community and to build new friendships.

For example, Susan, a ninety year-old with some spring in her step may enjoy leading a jazzy sing-a-long on the piano in the common sitting area. Joe may lead a hot game of poker where "the stakes are high and the refreshments are plenty."

Mary may love to teach her peers how to crochet blankets for the local children's hospital. Betty may enjoy sharing a family recipe and could invite a group to join her in preparing the dish. Mildred loves to walk and she could lead a group around the building every morning.

Joseph loves to read and used to be an English professor. He can get a book club together every Tuesday evening.

To assist the residents in leading activities, make sure there is a place for them to meet. Provide snacks and drinks. Post the activities on the board and makes regular announcements so everyone can attend the activities of their choice.

Chapter 10

Resident council

---

*E*ach community should have a council made up of residents. This council represents the wants and needs of the community. The meeting time should be scheduled once a month.

The residents have a right to meet as a group without staff involvement, however, they may invite a staff member to attend. A staff member cannot attend the meeting unless invited. There are council representatives that are voted in once per year. Those representatives are the voice of the residents as a whole. They bring concerns to the appropriate staff member such the executive director.

A notebook is kept with all the minutes of the resident council meeting. This notebook must be available to state surveyors.

Chapter 11

Building community relationships

The merchants in your community are interested in giving back. They tend to give to children's organizations because they are unaware of the needs of other groups. Start by introducing yourself. Build a personal relationship with the merchants and tell them about your Life Enrichment program before you make any requests. Do not just go in and ask for merchandise and supplies.

Personally invite the merchants to be a guest at any of your events. Once they enjoy themselves, they will keep coming back.

When you have a big event in the community and you have residents without family, ask the merchants to adopt a resident to sit with during the event.

Keep the merchants updated. Let them know their efforts are making a difference in the lives of the seniors.

Invite the merchants in to share their expertise such as the florist coming in to teach a flower arranging class, and the chef at Olive Garden coming in to teach a cooking class.

Write to their corporate office to let the administrators know of their staff's contributions.

Feature any community member who's contributed in your newsletter and give him a copy.

Hold a Community Appreciation Event. Have the residents make personalized gifts to thank the merchants for their time and contributions. Give the residents an opportunity to meet and greet. The merchants can spend time getting to know the residents on a more personal level. Give them an appreciation certificate. Invite the mayor and the media. Make it a really big deal.

Check with local super markets for clearance items they want to pass on. Send out photos of the residents using the supplies or goods passed onto the senior community.

Chapter 12

Bridging the generations

An example of a successful community event that has gone national

Assisted Living Senior Prom:
Behind the Scenes By Terri L. Glimcher

About four years ago, I started the *Bridging the Generations* program with the local schools in my city. I've worked with several teachers on an ongoing basis over the years to bring the two generations together. For the first visit, the children came to Oak Park to "Meet and Greet" my residents for the first visit. They were paired up with the residents and prepared to ask questions and listen to the wonderful stories the residents had to tell. The children were amazed! "Wow, you rode in a horse and buggy to school?", one child asked. The kids began to look at the residents as individuals.

Often times, children are afraid of seniors and view them as old, frail and vulnerable. This program really brings them inside the lives of seniors. They begin to see that aging is something to look forward to, not something to be afraid of. It is a part of life that we all experience. It's what you make of it that counts.

The second visit I have with the children is when I bring my residents into their high school. The children cook and serve breakfast to my residents. Last year, East Ridge High School students cooked a huge Thanksgiving dinner for the residents. The student band came in and played for them. The drama club, which consisted of the students that are in our program, performed a musical for them. Afterwards, the residents spent time listening to the students read speeches on what they were thankful for, and the students listened intently to what the seniors were thankful for.

The seniors saw first hand the art of text messaging, clothing that wasn't tailored, and multiple piercings. At first, I think they were shocked as to why a mother would let her child go out looking like that! Then as the students sat down with my residents, the residents began to look past the students' outer appearance. The elders began to have a deep appreciation for the students and understood it was a struggle for independence. The residents gave the kids advice about the importance of education, following their dreams, and to not judge a book by its cover. High school kids usually don't listen to adults, but for some reason, the children listened to the seniors.

The students learned firsthand about segregation. They learned it both from seniors who had to be at the back of the bus, and from the ones that could only play with friends who were white. The students were amazed that segregation was really a part of history. It was a very moving experience for both generations.

The relationship between the residents and the students is continuing to grow. We are involved with them once a week and many other times during the month. New schools continually want to be a part of this program. The kids also come and visit my residents all the time outside of school. They bake for them, are pen-pals with them and come to all of our dances.

My residents' faces light up when they see the kids. And the kids cannot run fast enough through the door to hug and kiss my residents. This program will continue for years to come for a simple reason: as much as the kids brighten the residents' days, the residents have enriched the lives of the children in the very same way. It is very important for children to step back in time and learn about life before the comforts of today. We want to teach them to not be afraid of growing old but to appreciate the lessons they've learned. We want them to understand that life as we know it now was pioneered by those who lived before us. It is our responsibility to teach children to respect and appreciate the elderly, and I will continue to do my part to bring the generations together.

On February 26, the high school students at Ocoee High School and East Ridge High School made the senior residents at Oak Park's dream of having a "Senior Prom" come true.

Every resident had a prom date from the high school. The residents were picked up at 5:30 p.m at their apartments, pinned with corsages and escorted to the photographer where prom pictures of the couples were taken. Following the photos the residents were escorted to the lobby where DJ Larry spun the tunes for the evening.

I would like to share with you some of the "behind-the-scenes-secrets" prior to and following the prom:

I arrived at work the morning of the 26th at 7:00 a.m. Five residents dressed in their gowns greeted me. I stated to them that the prom was not until 5:30 p.m.. They said they wanted to make sure they were not late for this event. "You should never keep a man waiting!" they said. These "men" are seventeen-year-old students.

We had Mary Kay representatives doing the residents' make up for the prom. Eleanor said, "I feel like a princess tonight." She is 89 years old.

She said, "I hope my date is 6'4" and handsome and I hope he has a lot of money!"

She got her wish. Her date was 6'3" and very handsome but... he's 17 and works at Dairy Queen! I guess two out of three isn't too bad, right?

The daughters and sons of the residents came in and dressed their family members. They waited in their rooms until their loved ones were picked up by their dates. On the way out the door, the families reminded their loved ones to be sure and call when they got home. Just like a normal prom, the families need to know that they made it home safely. The funny part is their rooms are twenty-five feet from the lobby.

I received a call at 8:30 p.m. from a resident's daughter. She said, "I'm worried sick, I thought mother would be home by now. She gets so tired."

I told her that her mother was fine and having fun. What she didn't know was that her mother was on the dance floor doing the "Electric Slide", the "Macarena", the "YMCA" arm movements and "The Twist" since 6:00 p.m. without sitting down once!

One of my favorite moments was when a resident named Pearl arrived with a beautiful dress on. As she came downstairs to the prom with her date, she lifted her skirt above the knee. There it was – a dime taped to her leg. As she showed me, I asked, "What are you going to do with that?" She said, "I need it here in case I need to make a phone call. My mother always told me to keep that dime under my dress." The prom was in our lobby, so I wasn't quite sure whom she was going to call, but I said, "That's a wonderful idea! You never know when you may need that."

The funniest comment of the night came from a high school student. He said "Miss Terri, these residents are running circles around us. We are tired! Do they ever stop dancing?"

Out of the mouths of babes!

Finally, the most moving moment was when one of the residents stated, "This is my first prom. We were poor. I never finished high school so I never went to the prom. This is the greatest day of my life! Thank you for making this prom happen. I will never ever forget this day as long as God will have me on this earth." She kissed and hugged me and cried.

Seventy residents and seventy-five students were in attendance as well as merchants from our community. The mayor of Clermont also attended. There was so much laughter and many tears flowed as the children nurtured the seniors as if they were gentle flowers. Overall, it was an amazing experience for the high school teachers, the staff, and the entire community.

It has always fascinated me how children in schools are taught history, but have never really met face-to-face with those who experienced or contributed to it. The older generation has been minimally exposed to modern technology such as computers, cell phones or iPods. They remember the old Victrola, entertainment through radio, the milkman delivering products, and the terrible Depression that we've only heard about on the news. I thought it would be a great idea to somehow bring the two generations together.

The seniors would learn about life the way it is for the children today, and the children would learn about what life was like when the seniors were growing up eighty to one hundred years ago.

Chapter 13

How to adapt an activity program

Continue to meet needs as residents decline in their abilities

*E*nlist the assistance of volunteers or other residents and have them help the declining resident participate. Only assist where necessary. Allow the person to keep his dignity.

Be flexible and willing to make changes as the need arises. Consider the following accommodations and use them where necessary:

- Shorten the duration of activities
- Books on tape
- Large print cards
- Bowling ramp
- Large print books

- Card shufflers
- Cardholders
- Change the cooking requirements from fine motor movements such as cutting with a knife, to broader movements such as stirring with a large spoon.
- Give reminders more often to come to activities
- Tape reminders to their walkers
- Use chair exercises if they can't stand
- Add an extra step to be able to step up on the van

Use your space efficiently and effectively. Always be aware of safety, such as the proper use of walkers. Make sure that people in power chairs are checked by home health agencies to ensure that the chairs are being used successfully.

Above all, listen to what the seniors are saying. Be especially aware that as residents decline physically, their mental capacities may also decline. It's not unusual for your most spunky residents to lose their energy levels and their memory.

When residents know their health and memory is declining, it is very upsetting. Do what you can to help ease their concerns. Remind them that you are there to help them if that does happen, and that they are in a safe environment.

When conversing with residents, don't use phrases like, "Remember when we...?", or "You already told me that." If memory is declining, these statements or questions only add to their frustration.

Residents with dementia appear to do really well with repetitive activities. Set up stations within the memory care area to represent tasks residents used to do when they were younger. These stations can include sewing machines, dress up with hats, beads, costume jewelry, non-toxic make-up, realistic baby dolls to care for and dress up, woodworking, repair stations with old radios, or other items to be "fixed", planting areas, and washing and drying laundry, are very good activities to start with. You will likely create new stations based on the individual needs of your community.

It is important to keep the activities brief since the residents' attention span has diminished. Higher staff to resident ratio is also important. Keep safety in mind and be sure that tools and equipment are safe to use and that no harm can come to any residents by accidentally ingesting materials.

Whereas it may be condescending to seniors with full mental capacity to use baby dolls or participate in activities that don't necessarily serve a functional purpose, the purpose of these stations is to recreate familiar activities from the past that allow the residents to feel successful in their everyday lives.

Additional activities for residents with dementia

These activities should be basic, should include very few residents, and should include many sensory and repetitive activities. Pair the "higher functioning" residents with residents who are having difficulties. Ensure that everyone is successful. Include music, simple basic dance, musical instruments, and sing-a-longs:

- Ice cube painting- freeze cool aid on a stick and let them paint with it
- Feely bag- fill it with textures
- Hokey pokey

- Scarf dancing- each resident is given a scarf and it is swayed to the music
- Planting
- Basic cooking
- Sponge painting
- Bingo doppers painting
- Bowling
- Horse shoes
- Ring toss
- Bacci Ball
- Interactive water activities
- Make snacks
- Bubbles

Chapter 14

How to incorporate the family

---

*I*nvolvement of family members will enhance your program. Make sure you connect with family members before the new resident arrives. Be personable and establish a relationship from the beginning. Interview the children or grandchildren to find out information about the new resident regarding his likes or dislikes regarding activities. What did the senior participate in when he was younger? Were there clubs or memberships he was a part of?

Most families really want to stay connected with their loved ones. One of the biggest fears is that their loved one is going to be lonely and spending time by herself. Assure them that most residents participate in the life enrichment program and then send photos of their loved one having a great time with their new friends in the activity room.

Keep the family involved and updated by using technology such as "Skype" where family members can talk and see each other through a camera set up on a computer.

Email is another way to stay in touch. Family members can stay connected through messages and quick notes.

Allow residents to have access to a phone if there is not one located in their room. It can be very frightening for the residents if they feel they're losing contact with their family

Invite the family to special events such as a fashion show. The residents can be the models and the family members can escort them down the red carpet.

Invite the family to a potluck dinner. Ask the family members to bring favorite family recipes such as grandma's apple pie or other special recipes that can bring back fond memories.

Invite families to share a talent. Family members are great volunteers. They can come in and lead bridge, cooking class, jewelry making, magic tricks, harp playing, a red hat's club, or a high tea party.

Create a recipe book using family recipes. Families contribute their recipes and the residents can put them together into a book form.

Chapter 15

Media

Connecting to media sources

Contact your local TV, and radio stations. Request the fax number and send press releases detailing your events with detailed information. Let them know why it should be covered. What makes this event important news?

Call your local newspaper. Ask them to have a local reporter cover your events such as a Senior Prom, or other big event.

If the media chooses to cover your story, stay in contact with them. After the stories are covered, send them a thank you note and keep them updated as to what's happening in your program every four to six weeks.

Chapter 16

Entertainment

$\mathcal{A}$sk other senior communities in the area who they use. Have the entertainer perform the first time for free to see if she is a fit for your community. If it is a fit, negotiate a price. Let them know you have a budget. If they want the job, they will work with you, if not, move on. Remember not to wipe out your entire budget on one entertainer.

Many times family members have untapped talent and will perform for free. Just ask.

If you have entertainers that are not engaging the seniors, do not re-book. The residents want to be entertained not lulled to sleep. They can do that on their own.

Make sure each entertainer fills out a W-9 and fills out a contract before the first entertainment date.

"Entertainment" is a huge category. It can include so much. From singers, to musicians, the list is as long as your creative mind takes you. Look for magicians, puppeteers, dancers, school children performers, belly dancers, cub scout troops, theater departments, the Lions club and 55 Plus communities to get started.

The following are examples of thematic events:

1. **High Tea Party:** The families were sent invitations to a High Tea party. Any residents that did not have a family member was paired with a community member. All attendees were asked to wear hats. The residents made their own hats out of materials purchased through Oriental Trading. The basics were provided and the folks created their own headpieces. The High Tea party was called to take place at 12:00 and a variety of tea was served in fine china. Finger sandwiches, crumpets and pastries were served. The British National Anthem played in the background. Some ladies arrived in formal attire while others were dressed more casually. Every participant wore a hat whether store purchased or created by hand.

2. **Hawaiian Luau:** Invitations went out in the shape of leis. A succulent pig was roasting in the back yard while dancing and other festivities were taking place. Hula dancers entertained the residents and their families. Then everyone joined in the dancing and grass skirts fluttered about. Any shy participant got hula lessons and was incorporated into the gyrating crowd. Everyone was refreshed with Mai Tais with and without alcohol. After dancing and resting, the entire group feasted on roasted pig. Every person got a lei as a remembrance of the event.

3. **Chinese New Year:** Invitations went out in English with Chinese characters. Everyone was asked to wear red and gold. Those who owned Chinese attire were

asked to wear their themed garments. Folks who owned Chinese artifacts were asked to bring them as decorations. A banner was hung representing The Year of The Rat. The lobby was decorated with Chinese New Year symbols. The local Chinese restaurant provided the name of a Chinese troupe that performed the Lion Dance. A mouth-watering buffet included fried rice, chicken chow mein, egg rolls, chicken wings, ribs, Chinese dumplings and Chinese hot tea was presented. Epcot's China Pavilion sent over a representative to play the zheng, a beautiful sounding stringed instrument. The representative spoke about Chinese culture and used elaborate props in her presentation. Everyone in attendance received a red envelope with a dollar in it to give the holder good luck for the coming year.

4. **Cinco De Mayo:** This event was created for the residents only. The gathering started at one o'clock. A piñata was stuffed to the brim with goodies and residents had a chance to smash it apart as each had a turn in hitting the hanging donkey. After the goodies were dispersed, a Mariachi band came in and played lively tunes as the Margaritas flowed. The folks then had the opportunity to do the Mexican hat dance. Those that couldn't stand and dance moved their feet to the beat. Everyone was so tired by the end of the festivities, it was concluded that a siesta was in order. (No one drank the water.)

5. **Hoe Down:** This event incorporated the high school students. The students came in early dressed in cowboy hats, jeans, and bandanas. Some of the students decorated the lobby while others prepared snacks. The hired DJ played county western music and line dance music. The students danced with the resident seniors then offered them snacks and drinks.

The students were polite and cordial and the seniors had a wonderful time dancing. Even the folks that normally don't like to participate got out of their chairs and moved to the rhythm of the beat. All attendees had a whooping good time.

Chapter 17

Senior
self-management

Run workshops on a regular basis for the residents on health related issues such as good hygiene, keeping one's mind healthy, nutrition, and overall good health practices for seniors. Remind them that as we age, our needs change.

As a life enrichment partner, it will be necessary to speak to people about issues such as hygiene, behavior and health.

If you notice that residents have used the restroom but have not washed their hands, they need to be reminded about spreading germs and the importance of cleanliness, especially after using the restroom and before cooking or handling food.

Have tissues and hand sanitizer available at all times, and especially during flu season. (Check for allergies to the hand sanitizer.)

Have the residents bring extra incontinence supplies with them on trips outside the building.

If the residents have an odor or seem to be wet, call upon the CNAs or nursing staff to unobtrusively assist the residents in getting themselves clean so they can return back to activities as soon as possible.

If a resident doesn't seem to be attending to others, or to the activities, check his hearing aids. Any other concerns should be immediately reported to the nursing staff.

Chapter 18

Behavioral issues

$\mathscr{A}$s we go through life and reach our golden years, there are times that we get irritable. If residents are "grouchy" once in a while, that is okay. Politely remind them of the expectations of treating one another with kindness.

Some people are irritable and mean on a regular basis. In this case, take the person aside and let him or her know that being rude or uncooperative is not conducive to activity time and if it continues he or she will be asked to leave the activity room. It is also imperative that the nursing staff is apprised of the situation and the person's medications are reviewed and their overall physical well-being is checked. Remember, we are a team. Keep the staff up to date on behavior changes and physical changes.

It may be necessary to inform the family members of the unwanted behavior to keep them updated and to pull in their support. Another option is to remove the resident from the scheduled activity. If the person refuses, you may have to put an end to the activity temporarily until the person begins to cooperate.

Chapter 19

Establishing friendships

As with any person coming into a new community, feeling connected is very important. When new people come into the community, assign a peer to be a "buddy". Try to have someone of like interests paired with the new person. Ask the veteran senior to invite the "newcomer" to activities and set them up to lead an activity together.

Chapter 20

When a fellow resident passes

*W*hen fellow residents decline and then pass, it is very emotional for their friends that are left behind. Often they see a friend declining and start to pull away because it makes them question their own fate. The residents also become less patient when they see others "going downhill". There are expectations that the person who is declining be as on top of things as she was when she first arrived.

Make sure you have the wherewithal to assist these folks as they decline. You too have to be extra patient. You may have to explain and re-explain that you are there to help everyone no matter the state he or she is in, and as a community it is up to everyone to assist one another in making it through difficult times.

When a peer passes on, be honest with the group and let them know that someone has passed. Be aware of HIPPA laws and do not give out and medical or personal information. On the other hand, allow time for grief. Letters can be written to family and arrangements can be made to attend services.

Don't pretend the death didn't happen or be light about it as if it's "just a fact of life", be compassionate and empathetic. You may see behavior changes in residents after the passing. They are likely wondering if they'll be next or maybe they just feel the loss of a friend and need time to adjust.

Chapter 21

Creating a memory book

From the time a resident comes in. We start a memory book. The memory book is a compilation of photos, notes, letters to family members, a memoir of the legacy he wants to leave, likes and dislikes, a history of careers and service involvement, and any other memorabilia that he chooses to leave for his family.

Chapter 22

Preparing for
end of life

The Life Enrichment program is just that. The focus is on enriching the life of the seniors as they live out their golden years. However, as a resident is facing death, it is important to support the family members. The family may be staying with their declining loved one in their apartment. Hospice may have been called as the family prepares for their last goodbyes.

Allow the family to give out information to other residents. Do not divulge any information that would breach the HIPPA law.

Remember to offer the family snacks or a break from sitting with their loved one. Be a listener and offer compassion. On the other hand, some families prefer privacy. In this case, just be available if they call upon you. You may not think this is part of your job, however, as a partner with your residents, you have become an integral part of their everyday life, and you may be an integral part of a resident passing on.

FAMILY RESOURCES

Chapter 23

Looking for an assisted living community

For the folks who feel comfortable with the use of a computer, use a search engine such as "Google" and type in "assisted living". Put in your city and state to narrow down the possibilities. The Department of Elder Affairs, The Department of Children and Families, and The Veterans Association are also good resources.

Once you find some possible facilities, start touring. Trust your heart. If it doesn't feel good, don't leave your parent there.

Set up an appointment to see the facility and take the tour they offer. Then take some time to talk to some of the residents. Ask them about the program and get their feedback. Notice the surroundings. Is the building clean? Is the staff attentive to the needs of the residents? Request to eat a meal in the dining facility. Notice the service, the quality of the food and the surroundings. Is this a place you would like to eat three times a day? Is the director friendly and personable or all business? Are people sitting around falling asleep in chairs or are they engaged in activities?

While the living area is extremely important, I feel there are three main topics that must be taken in consideration when choosing a facility for your loved one to live out his or her golden years.

First, the food must be tasty and of good quality. Is the staff cognizant of the dietary needs of the residents? Is the food hot and served quickly? Do people have space to move around and is the environment conducive to a relaxed eating experience?

Second, is the medical staff attentive to the individual needs of the residents? Are they moving about and checking on people or are they standing around looking bored?

Third, is the activity program interesting and engaging? Sit in on a scheduled activity and look at the schedule to see what is being offered for the week.

If these main ingredients are in place and are of good quality, most of the other pieces will fall into place.

How to Interview an Activity Director

The following is an article written by Terri Glimcher and was featured by "InsideElderCare.com", an online resource for families:

Having been an activity director for four years, I truly enjoy when families collaborate on a plan to get their loved ones involved in the activities in my community.

When first touring an assisted living community, it is very important to receive a copy of the activities calendar. Most seniors who are transitioning to assisted living have been very active in their communities prior to the transition.

It is very important that they continue to be active and feel a part of their community. Here are some recommendations to make that more likely.

Meet the Activity Director

Ask to meet with the activity director. Let the activity director know what kind of activities your loved one really enjoys. If those activities are not a part of their program, ask them how they can incorporate the things your loved one enjoys into the weekly routine.

Get Out of the Building

Make sure residents are taken out into the community for activities. Staying on the assisted living grounds all the time is not an acceptable option. Ask your activities director if and how they are connected to the community. Many times during the transition period, residents prefer to remain isolated in their rooms. The activities director should be able to clearly articulate the ways he or she plans to help your loved one connect with other residents.

In my facility, I have a welcome committee made up of residents that greet a new resident immediately and will stay close to them during the transition. They will come get them for meals, activities, and just spend time connecting with them on a personal level. This has been very helpful in transitioning and integrated new residents into the "family."

Physical, Cognitive and Emotional Stimulation

Ask your activity director how he or she plans to meet the physical, cognitive and emotional needs of your loved ones.

If your loved one has a disability — physical, vision, hearing or dementia — ask the activity director how activities are adapted so that your loved one may participate.

Your loved one should never be left out because the activities cannot be adapted to his needs. This should be an important factor in your community selection process. Every activity in my program can be modified to meet the needs of every resident in our community.

I have a simple rule: **If it can't be adapted, we don't do it.**

Stay Connected with Long-Distance Families

Many families live far away from the community where their loved one resides. Ask the activity director how you can stay connected with them and how you stay informed about their participation in the activities program. I do this through pictures and emails. I send pictures of the residents participating in their activities to the families.

Activities for Individuals

I have several residents who prefer not to do physical activities or crafts. In their younger years they owned a store or did floral arranging, so I opened a General Store in our community. These residents take a great deal of pride in taking inventory and working as the cashier within our community. Ask your activity director if he or she is willing to add activities for individual residents to help them feel apart of their surroundings. The most important factor is that your loved ones have a purpose. They need to be stimulated every day — physically, cognitively and emotionally.

Communication is Key

The activity director should provide a "safe space" for your loved one to be able to come to talk, participate or just to come for a hug. Communication should occur on a regular basis with the families, either by phone, email or mail. Follow up with your activity director to make sure your loved one is participating and is not isolated.

A Successful Program is Obvious

A healthy program has a consistent flow of activities from morning until early evening. Healthy programs have a variety of choices. Families may even want to participate and join an activity with their loved one.

I have 8 activities a day with 40- 50 participants engaged daily.

Look for these qualities in an activity program and be assured that your loved one will be kept stimulated cognitively, physically, and emotionally.

Chapter 24

Activities for aging loved ones that will continue to live on their own or with family members

---

$\mathcal{M}$any families prefer to have an aging loved one stay at their own home with support or will have a senior family member move in with their children or grandchildren. Whether the reason is financial or cultural, there are times that providing care can be overwhelming. Remember that even the most patient and loving family members can get tired and burned out. Not only are they caring for their own children, many adults are now also taking care of their parents. If this is your situation, take care of yourself also. Have a trusted friend or relative stay with your elderly loved one while you take time to get rested and refreshed. If you become tired and frustrated, it will be more difficult to interact with your parents or grandparents in the way you both deserve. This is especially important if your loved one is becoming more dependent or is showing signs of dementia.

The following are suggestions to make your time together more pleasant and fulfilling:

1. **Create a daily routine.** Be consistent throughout. Keep wake up and meal times the same. Plan outings at the same time each day. Changes will happen and you must be prepared to the best of your ability, however, knowing what to expect and following a routine makes the day go easier for your senior adult.

2. **When planning a daily or weekly activity list, make sure the schedule allows some time outdoors and time in the community.** A nice walk or an outing to an eatery will really enhance their day. Another trip can include going to the local library. This is a great resource that is plentiful an inexpensive. It's heated in the winter and air conditioned in the summer. There are accommodations for folks who are visually impaired. Books on tape or large print text are options. Once the librarian gets to know you, he or she will be glad to have special interest books on hand when you arrive. There are also many free events that you can build into your regular schedule.

3. **Allow your loved ones to help in meal preparation.** Cooking is a wonderful activity that has delicious results. Parents will often remember the savory or sweet smells which can bring back fond memories. Skills that may have been lost may come back when in the food preparation process. Since cooking is so versatile, you can get very detailed or keep it very simple.

   One way to make cooking a full day activity is to watch a cooking show. Use the recipe presented and go over it with your loved one. Check through the pantry and refrigerator for needed supplies. Make a list of the missing items. Go to the store with a checklist and find the necessary ingredients. Come home, gather the supplies, lay out the bowls and utensils needed and follow the recipe. Enjoy the process. Each step will lead to the desired result; an enjoyable activity with a tasty ending.

To keep it simple, it may be necessary to have most of the preparation done ahead of time. Have your parent assist with whatever he or she is able to. Perhaps she will only mix the ingredients. Maybe he will help with the chopping. The point is to allow an involvement level that works for the both of you. Sometimes this will take experimenting. As you know, some days are better than others. Try to pick a "good" day so the both of you will be left fulfilled rather than frustrated.

When looking for cooking activities, simply go to a user friendly search engine such as "Google" and type in "no bake desserts", or "simple recipes". You will find hundreds of resources. Using "no bake" recipes is one way to prevent a loved one from having to use the stove-top or oven and can prevent possible safety issues from occurring. *Note: some no bake recipes do call for melting on the stove top. Simply use the recipe that fits your needs.

Ten websites are listed below which feature simple or no bake recipes:

http://www.realsimple.com/food-recipes

http://allrecipes.com

http://www.foodnetwork.com/quick-and-easy

http://easy-recipes.hypermart.net

http://www.cooks.com/rec/search/0,1-0,easy_to_make
_food,FF.html

http://allrecipes.com//Recipes/desserts/cookies/no-bake
-cookies/Main.aspx

http://www.cooksrecipes.com/cookies/no-bake-cookie
-recipes.html

http://www.christmas-cookies.com/recipes/nobakecookies
.html?curl=nobake

http://www.delish.com/recipes/cooking-recipes/quick-no
-cook-dinner-recipes

http://www.rachaelraymag.com/Recipes/special-recipe
-collections/easy-ideas-no-bake-desserts

4. **If mom or dad is having incontinence issues your outings may need to be shorter.** They can remain just as effective. A trip to your local fruit stand for some fresh fruit can make a pleasant short outing. A ride to the lake to feed the ducks or a jaunt to the airport to watch the planes can be fun, short activities.

5. **Utilize your local churches, VFW, high school, and colleges to enlist volunteers to come to your home.** Do background checks if you feel uncomfortable or get references from others they've volunteered with. Volunteers are great sources of activities and can play chess, board games, take mom or dad to a sporting event, a movie, or just sit down and have a chat. This will free up some time for you to get the things done you need to do. Sharing the responsibilities does not mean that you are neglecting their needs. Sharing allows others to contribute to the success of your loved

one's golden years. New and refreshing experiences definitely enhance your activity schedule.

6. **Ask your local church to pick up mom or dad if they are able and take her or him to worship services.**

7. **If grandchildren are a part of the environment, make sure they are interacting with their grandparent at some point.** Include the very young and older grandchildren. They are a wealth of knowledge. They can teach grandma or grandpa how to use computers, how to use a cell phone and how to do the latest dances. Grandparents get great pleasure out of sharing in the grandchildren's lives even if its only for a short time.

8. **Try to let your loved one be as independent as possible.** Often times in the latter years seniors prefer that we do things for them. They are not willing to try new things or help themselves. Sometimes they just give up when they've lost their independence. They may have a decreased desire to live and they do not want to burden their children. Keeping them active and involved will make a difference in this area. Once a person feels useless he or she will give up. You can help prevent this from happening.

9. **Watch for signs of depression, lack of motivation, loss of appetite, changes in overall mood, changes in hygiene and any other behaviors that are out of the ordinary.** Consult a physician and get the support you need to keep your family healthy both mentally and physically.

Chapter 25

Adult Day Care

---

*A*dult day care is another option for your family member. Day programs are offered to keep your loved ones stimulated. Interactive scheduling is important to engage one's body and mind. Interview the director and make sure the center provides not only "busy work", but activities that include the various needs of the clientele. Bingo, crafts, trivia, exercise, music and movement, and off property trips should be incorporated in the schedule. If the focus is on television and movies only, look somewhere else.

Does the program encourage friendships? Socialization is of utmost importance and will allow your parent or grandparent the opportunity to connect to peers.

Find out if lunch is provided and if it meets the special dietary needs of your family member.

What are their emergency procedures? Is there a medically trained staff member available if needed?

Does the program provide transportation to community events?

Is there an area and opportunity to rest if needed?

Does the center offer evening programs? This is a great opportunity to get some personal time and to pamper yourself.

If you keep these basic points in mind and if you trust your instincts, you will find an appropriate place for your loved one.

Chapter 26

Skilled Nursing, Nursing Homes, (SNF, Skilled Nursing Facility)

*W*hen your loved one needs more assistance than assisted living or memory care can provide, a skilled nursing home may be an option for you. The higher ratio of staff to patients allows for more intensive care. Start looking at both assisted and skilled nursing facilities as soon as you notice a decline. There is often a waiting list to get into the most reputable ones. Settling is not an option.

Finding exactly what is best for your loved one makes the transition go much smoother.

It is important when you look into skilled nursing facilities to make sure you check with the health department and ask to see their most recent state surveys. This will tell you if they've had any violations and in what areas the violations occurred.

If the facility is acceptable to you and your family, take time to meet with the activity director. Find out how he or she will incorporate your loved one's needs and wants into their programs. Can they adapt the program to meet your needs?

Observe the activity program and take note. Are activities going on throughout the day? Are residents participating? Have accommodations been made to fit the needs of all involved?

Keep in mind that this setting is often very different from where your loved one had lived prior to the move. It may take time to adjust to the new setting. Sometimes residents choose to remain isolated because they are experiencing depression. In order to help with the transition, go with your loved one to some activities until he or she feels up to going on his or her own.

Once you attend an activity, ask the director to introduce your parent to someone with similar interests or someone she can befriend.

Make the atmosphere more homelike and inviting by brightening the room with memories of children and grandchildren. Have the kids make pictures to put on the walls.

Frequent visits are always helpful. Oftentimes folks feel as if they will be "left" there or forgotten. Even folks with dementia know that someone comes to visit them. Keep your visits consistent. Remain an advocate and stay on top of the care they receive. Sometimes our loved ones cannot speak for themselves. We need to be their voice.

Resources for families and life enrichment directors

Information on the latest issues concerning seniors
http://www.insideeldercare.com

Reverend Linn Possell, BS, MS, Mdiv is a counselor for life transitions. She specializes in dealing with loved ones with dementia. RevPossell@gmail.com

Highly recommended home health care agency in Ohio:
http://www.ElanHomeHealth.com

Highly recommeded hair salon to incorporate into your ALF, Independent or Skilled Nursing facility:
http://www.ElanSalonGroup.com

American Foundation for the Blind
http://www.afb.org

Assisted living Federation of America
http://www. alfa.org

Large Bingo Cards adaptive equipment
http://www.alliedbingo.com

Alzheimer's Association
http://www.alz.org

Activity resources:
http://www.theactivitydirectorsoffice.com

I'm on my own with nowhere to turn

The following are online resources and resources that can be contacted by telephone.

If you are in dire need of emergency medical help, dial 911 and wait to speak to the operator, otherwise seek assistance from the following resources:

A referral agency for assisted living, skilled nursing and memory care
http://www.aplaceformom.com

Senior Services
http://www.carepathways.com

U.S. Department of Health and Human Services
800-633-4227
http://www.cms.gov/LimitedIncomeandResources

U.S. Department of Veteran Affairs
http://www.VA.gov

The Official U.S. Government Site for Medicare
http://www.medicare.gov

Online access to food and human nutrition information
http://www.nutrition.gov

The Official Website of the U.S. Social Security Administration
1-800-772-1213
http://www.ssa.gov

The Home page for AARP
888-687-2277
http://www.aarp.org

U.S. Department of Housing and Urban Development
800-955-2232
http://portal.hud.gov

The Official Site of the National Association of Realtors
http://www.realtor.com

Meals on Wheels
http://www.mowaa.org

Florida Department of Elder Affairs
http://elderaffairs.state.fl.us

Florida Elder Helpline
1-800-96-ELDER

Report Elder Abuse
1-800-96-ABUSE

Florida State Senior Legal Helpline
1-888-895-7873

Report Elder Abuse		
State	**Domestic/Community**	**Nursing Home/Long Term Care Facility**
Alabama	1-800-458-7214 Alabama Adult Protective Services: http://www.dhr.state.al.us/page.asp?pageid=274	1-800-458-7214 Alabama Department of Senior Services: http://www.adss.state.al.us/elderabuse2.htm
Alaska	1-800-478-9996 (Toll free in Alaska) Outside of Alaska: 907-269-3666 Alaska Adult Protective Services: http://www.hss.state.ak.us/dsds/aps.htm	1-800-730-6393 (Toll free in Alaska) Outside of Alaska: 907-334-4483
Arizona	1-SOS-ADULT or 1-877-767-2385 602-674-4200 TDD: 1-877-815-8390 Arizona Adult Protective Services http://www.hss.state.ak.us/dsds/aps.htm	1-SOS-ADULT or 1-877-767-2385 602-674-4200 TDD: 1-877-815-8390

Report Elder Abuse		
Arkansas	1-800-332-4443 (Toll free in Arkansas) Outside of Arkansas: 1-800-482-8049 E-mail: Carolyn.singleton@ arkanas.gov Arkansas Domestic Violence/ Battered Women Hotline: 1-800-332-4443 Arkansas Adult Protective Services http://www .aradultprotection.com/	1-800-582-4887 In Pulaski County: 501-682-8425 Fax: 501-682-1967, Attention Complaint Unit E-mail: complaints.OLTC@ arkansas.gov Arkansas Office of Long Term Care, Complaints Unit http://www.medicaid. state.ar.us/InternetSolu- tion/General/units/oltc/ complaint.aspx Arkansas Long Term Care Ombudsman http://www.arombudsman. com/
California	1-888-436-3600 (Toll free in California) Outside of California: Call County Adult Protective Services California Adult Protective Services http://www.dss. cahwnet.gov/cdssweb/ Protective_175.htm	1-800-231-4024 California Long Term Care Ombudsman http://www.aging.state. ca.us/html/programs/ ombudsman.html

Report Elder Abuse		
Colorado	1-800-773-1366	1-800-773-1366 or
		1-800-886-7689, Ext. 2800
		(303) 692-2800
		E-mail: health.facilities@ state.co.us
		Fax: (303) 753-6214
		Colorado Department of Public Health Nursing Home Complaints Program
		http://www.cdphe.state. co.us/hf/static/ncfcomp. htm
Connecticut	1-888-385-4225 or 1-860-424-5241 After Hours/Emergency: 2-1-1 (In-State only) E-mail: lynn.noyes@ po.state.ct.us Connecticut Protective Services for the Elderly http://www.dss.state.ct.us/ svcs/socialwork/pg3.htm	1-860-424-5241
Delaware	1-800-223-9074 Delaware Adult Protective Services http://www.dhss.delaware. gov/dhss/dsaapd/aps.html	1-800-223-9074
District of Columbia	202-541-3950 DC Adult Protective Services http://www.dhss.delaware. gov/dhss/dsaapd/aps.html	202-434-2140

Report Elder Abuse		
Florida	1-800-96-ABUSE or 1-800-962-2873 TDD/TTY: 1-800-453-5145 Fax: 1-800-914-0004 Florida Adult Protective Services http://www.dcf.state.fl.us /as Florida Mandatory Reporter Fax Transmittal Form http://www.dcf.state.fl.us/ abuse/faxreport.pdf	1-800-96ABUSE or 1-800-962-2873
Georgia	1-888-774-0152 404-657-5250 (Metro-Atlanta) Georgia Adult Protective Services http://www.dfcs.dhr. georgia.gov/portal/site/ DHR-DFCS/menuitem.5d322 35bb09bde9a50c8798dd0303 6a0/?vgnextoid=83ea2b48d 9a4ff00VgnVCM100000bf010 10aRCRD	1-800-878-6442 404-657-5728 (Metro-Atlanta) Georgia Office of Regulatory Services http://dhr.georgia.gov/ portal/site/DHR/menuitem. 3d43c0fad7b3111b50c8798d d03036a0/?vgnextoid=efefc 35b0fb4ff00VgnVCM100000 bf01010aRCRD&vgnextcha nnel=b49807b35414ff00Vgn VCM100000bf01010aRCRD
Guam	671-475-0268 After Hours: 671-646-4455 (evenings, weekends, holidays)	671-475-0268 After Hours: 671-646-4455 (evenings, weekends, holidays)

Report Elder Abuse		
Hawaii	808-832-5115 (Oahu) 808-243-5151 (Maui, Molokai, and Lanai) 808-241-3432 (Kauai) 808-933-8820 (East Hawaii) 808-327-6280 (West Hawaii) Hawaii Executive Office on Aging http://www4.hawaii.gov/eoa/programs/response/report.html	808-832-5115(Oahu) 808-243-5151 (Maui, Molokai, and Lanai) 808-241-3432 (Kauai) 808-933-8820 (East Hawaii) 808-327-6280 (West Hawaii) Hawaii Long Term Care Ombudsman 808-586-0100
Idaho	1-877-471-2777 Idaho Adult Protection http://www.idahoaging.com/programs/ps_adultprotect.htm	1-877-471-2777
Illinois	1-800-252-8966 (Toll free in Illinois - Voice & TTY) Outside of Illinois: 217-524-6911 or 1-800-677-1116 (Eldercare Locator) After Hours Hotline: 1-800-279-0400 E-mail: ilsenior@aging.state.il Illinois Protective Services for Seniors http://www.state.il.us/aging/1abuselegal/abuse.htm Illinois Local Elder Abuse Provider AgencyDirectory http://www.state.il.us/aging/1helpline/helpline-main.htm	1-800-252-4343 (Toll free in Illinois) TTY: 1-800-547-0466 Outside of Illinois: 217-785-0321 http://www.state.il.us/aging/1abuselegal/ombuds_reporting.htm Illinois Department on Aging

Report Elder Abuse		
Indiana	1-800-992-6978 (Toll free in Indiana) Outside of Indiana: 1-800-545-7763, Ext. 20135 Indiana Adult Protective Services http://www.in.gov/fssa/elderly/aging/aps.html	1-800-992-6978 (Toll free in Indiana) Outside of Indiana: 1-800-545-7763, Ext. 20135
Iowa	1-800-362-2178 Iowa Department of Human Services http://www.dhs.state.ia.us/dhs2005/dhs_homepage/children_family/abuse_reporting/adult_abuse.html	1-877-686-0027 Iowa Long Term Care Ombudsman http://www.state.ia.us/elderaffairs/advocacy/ombudsman.html Iowa Department of Inspections and Appeals, Health Facilities Division http://www.state.ia.us/government/dia/page8.html
Kansas	1-800-922-5330 (Toll free in Kansas) Outside of Kansas: 785-296-0044 Kansas Adult Protective Services http://www.srskansas.org/ISD/ees/adult.htm	1-800-842-0078 1-877-662-8362 (Toll free in Kansas) Outside of Kansas: 785-296-3017 Kansas Office of the State Long Term Care Ombudsman http://da.state.ks.us/care/

Report Elder Abuse		
Kentucky	Elder Abuse Hotline: 1-800-752-6200 Spouse Abuse Hotline: 1-800-544-2022 Kentucky Cabinet for Health and Family Services http://chfs.ky.gov/dcbs/dpp/eaa/ Kentucky Adult Protective Services http://chfs.ky.gov/dcbs/dpp/facs.htm	Elder Abuse Hotline: 1-800-752-6200 Long Term Care Ombudsman: 1-800-372-2991 TTY (for hearing impaired): 1-800-627-4702 Attorney General's Patient Abuse Tip Line: 1-877-ABUSE TIP (1-877-228-7384) Office of the Attorney General Medicaid Fraud & Abuse Control Division http://ag.ky.gov/abuse/ Kentucky Office of Inspector General http://chfs.ky.gov/oig/dhcf-scomplaintinfo.htm
Louisiana	1-800-259-4990 (Toll free in Louisiana) Outside of Louisiana: 225-342-9722 Adults with Disabilities (Ages 18-59) 1-800-898-4910 Louisiana Elderly Protective Services http://louisiana.gov /elderlyaffairs/eps.htm	1-800-259-4990 (Toll free in Louisiana) Outside of Louisiana: 225-342-9722 Adults With Disabilities (Ages 18-59) 1-800-898-4910

Report Elder Abuse		
Maine	1-800-624-8404 (Toll free in Maine) Outside of Maine: 207-532-5047 or 207-287-6083 (After Hours) TTY: 1-800-624-8404 TTY After Hours (In-State) 1-800-963-9490 TTY After Hours (Out-of-State) 207-287-3492 Maine Bureau of Elder and Adult Services http://www.maine.gov/dhhs/beas/aps.htm	1-800-383-2441 (Toll free in Maine) Local/Out-of-State TTY: 207-287-9312 Maine Department of Health and Human Services http://www.maine.gov/dhhs/beas/resource/anequide.htm
Maryland	1-800-917-7383 (Toll free in Maryland) Outside of Maryland: 1-800-677-1116 (Eldercare Locator) Maryland Adult Protective Services http://www.dhr.state.md.us/how/srvadult/protect.htm	1-800-917-7383 (Toll free in Maryland) 1-800-AGE-DIAL, Ext. 1091 (Toll free in Maryland) Outside of Maryland: 410-767-1091 Maryland Long Term Care Ombudsman/Elder Abuse Prevention http://www.mdoa.state.md.us/Services/Ombudsman.html

Report Elder Abuse		
Massachusetts	1-800-922-2275 (Toll free in Massachusetts - Voice/TTY) Outside of Massachusetts: 1-800-AGE-INFO (1-800-243-4636) TDD/TTY: 1-800-872-0166 Massachusetts Elder Protection Services and Programs http://www.sec.state.ma.us/cis/ciscig/o/o6o15.htm	1-800-462-5540 1-800-AGE-INFO (1-800-243-4636) Massachusetts Attorney General's Elder Hotline: 1-888-AG-ELDER (1-888-243-5337) TTY: 617-727-0434
Michigan	1-800-996-6228 Michigan Adult Protective Services http://www.michigan.gov/dhs/0,1607,7-124-5452_7119-15663--,00.html	1-800-882-6006 Michigan Bureau of Health Systems http://www.michigan.gov/mdch/0,1607,7-132-27417_28139_28142---,00.html
Minnesota	1-800-333-2433 TDD/TYY: 1-800-627-3529 Minnesota Aging Protective Services Unit http://www.dhs.state.mn.us/main/groups/aging/documents/pub/dhs_id_005710.hcsp	1-800-333-2433 TDD/TYY: 1-800-627-3529
Mississippi	1-800-222-8000 (Toll free in Mississippi) Outside of Mississippi: (601) 359-4991 E-Mail: webspinner@mdhs.state.ms.us Mississippi Adult Protective Services http://www.mdhs.state.ms.us/fcs_aps.html	1-800-227-7308 1-800-222-8000 (Toll free in Mississippi) Outside of Mississippi: (601) 359-4991

Report Elder Abuse		
Missouri	• 1-800-392-0210 More Information Missouri Adult Protective Services http://www.health.state. mo.us/ProtectiveServices/	• 1-800-392-0210
Montana	• 1-800-551-3191 (Toll free in Montana) • Outside of Montana: 406-444-4077 More Information Montana Adult Protective Services http://www.dphhs.state. mt.us/sltc/protective_ legal/07.02.adulprot.servs. htm	• 1-800-551-3191 (Toll free in Montana) • Outside of Montana: 406-444-4077 More Information Montana Senior & Long Term Care Division Ombudsman http://www.dphhs.mt.gov/ sltc/index.htm
Nebraska	• 1-800-652-1999 (Toll free in Nebraska) • Outside of Nebraska: 402-595-1324 More Information Nebraska Adult Protective Services http://www.hhs.state. ne.us/ags/aps.htm	• 1-800-652-1999 (Toll free in Nebraska) • Outside of Nebraska: 402-595-1324

Report Elder Abuse		
Nevada	1-800-992-5757 (Toll free in Nevada) Outside of Nevada: Carson City area: 775-687-4210 Reno area: 775-688-2964 Elko area: 775-738-1966 Las Vegas area: 702-486-3545 Nevada Elder Protective Services http://www.nvaging.net/protective_svc.htm	1-800-992-5757 (Toll free in Nevada) Outside of Nevada: Carson City area: 775-687-4210 Reno area: 775-688-2964 Elko area: 775-738-1966 Las Vegas area: 702-486-3545
New Hampshire	1-800-351-1888 or 603-271-4680 After Hours: 911 or local police after hours, weekends, or holidays New Hampshire Adult Protection Program http://www.dhhs.state.nh.us/DHHS/BEAS/adult-protection.htm	1-800-442-5640 or 603-271-4375 New Hampshire Office of the Long Term Care Ombudsman
New Jersey	1-800-792-8820 (Toll free in New Jersey) Outside of New Jersey: 609-943-3473 E-mail: acs@doh.state.nj.us New Jersey Adult Protective Services http://www.state.nj.us/health/senior/aps.shtml	1-800-792-8820 (Toll free in New Jersey) Outside of New Jersey: 609-943-3473 E-mail: acs@doh.state.nj.us
New Mexico	1-800-797-3260 or 505-841-6100 (In Albuquerque	1-800-797-3260 or 505-841-6100 (In Albuquerque)

Report Elder Abuse		
New York	1-800-342-3009 (Toll free in New York) - Press Option 6 New York Protective Services for Adults http://www.ocfs.state.ny.us/main/psa/	NURSING HOME COMPLAINTS 1-888-201-4563 E-Mail: nhintake@health.state.ny.us ADULT CARE HOME COMPLAINTS 866-893-6772 New York State Department of Health Nursing Homes http://www.health.state.ny.us/facilities/nursing/ Adult Care Facilities http://www.health.state.ny.us/facilities/adult_care/
North Carolina	1-800-662-7030 North Carolina Adult Protective Services http://www.dhhs.state.nc.us/aging/adultsvcs/afs_aps.htm	1-800-662-7030
North Dakota	1-800-451-8693 North Dakota Vulnerable Adult Protective Services	1-800-451-8693
Ohio	866-635-3748 (Toll free in Ohio) Outside of Ohio: 1-800-677-1116 (Eldercare Locator) Ohio Adult Protective Services http://www.goldenbuckeye.com/aps.html	1-800-342-0533 TDD: 614-752-6490 Fax: 614-728-9169 E-mail: HCComplaints@gw.odh.state.oh.us Ohio Department of Health http://www.odh.ohio.gov/odhPrograms/dspc/complnt/complnt1.aspx

Report Elder Abuse		
Oklahoma	1-800-522-3511 Oklahoma Adult Protective Services http://www.okdhs.org/APS/contactus.html	
Oregon	1-800-232-3020 TTY/Voice: 503-945-5811 Oregon Adult Protective Services http://www.oregon.gov/DHS/spwpd/abuse/home.shtml	1-800-522-2602 or 503-378-6533 AGING/DEVELOPMENTAL DISABILITIES 1-800-866-406-4287 or 503-945-9495 Oregon Long Term Care Ombudsman http://www.oregon.gov/LTCO/services.shtml Oregon Department of Human Services Office of Investigations http://www.dhs.state.or.us/disabilities/developmental_disabilities/abuse/reporting_abuse.htm
Pennsylvania	1-800-490-8505 Pennsylvania Protective Services for Adults http://www.aging.state.pa.us/aging/cwp/view.asp?A=284&Q=173897	1-800-254-5164 Pennsylvania Department of Health http://www.dsf.health.state.pa.us/health/
Puerto Rico	787-725-9788 or 787-721-8225	

Report Elder Abuse		
Rhode Island	401-462-0550	401-785-3340
	Fax: 401-462-0545	Fax: 401-785-3391
	Rhode Island Department of Elderly Affairs Protective Services Unit http://www.dea.ri.gov/ programs/protective_ services.php	
South Carolina	803-898-7318	803-898-2850
	South Carolina Adult Protective Services http://www.state.sc.us/dss/ aps/	
South Dakota	605-773-3656	605-773-3656
	South Dakota Adult Protective Services http://www.state.sd.us/ social/ASA/Services/ protective/	
	Online Referral/Request https://www.state.sd.us/ social/ASA/Forms/Intake/ intake.htm	
	South Dakota local adult protection offices https://www.state.sd.us/ social/ASA/Forms/Intake/ intake.htm	

Report Elder Abuse		
Tennessee	1-888-APS-TENN or 1-888-277-8366 Knoxville: (865) 594-5685 Chattanooga: (423) 634-6624 Nashville: (615) 532-3492 Memphis: (901) 320-7220 Tennessee Adult Protective Services http://www.tennessee.gov/humanserv/adpro.htm	1-888-APS-TENN or 1-888-277-8366
Texas	1-800-252-5400 (Toll free in Texas) Outside of Texas: 512-834-3784 Texas Adult Protective Services http://www.dfps.state.tx.us/Adult_Protection/About_Adult_Protective_Services/ Online Abuse/Neglect/Exploitation Reporting Form https://www.txabusehotline.org/PublicMain.asp	1-800-458-9858 (Toll free in Texas) Outside of Texas: 512-834-3784
Utah	1-800-371-7897 (Toll free in Utah) Outside of Utah: 801-264-7669 E-mail: vruesch@utah.gov Utah Adult Protective Services http://www.hsdaas.utah.gov/ap_referral.htm	1-800-371-7897 (Toll free in Utah) Outside of Utah: 801-264-7669 E-mail: vruesch@utah.gov

Report Elder Abuse		
Vermont	1-800-564-1612 802-241-2345 Fax: 802-241-2358 Vermont Adult Protective Services http://www.dad.state.vt.us/lp/aps.htm APS Online Report Form http://www.dad.state.vt.us/lp/New APS Pages/reportingform.htm	1-800-564-1612 802-241-2345 Fax:802-241-2358 More Information APS Online Report Form http://www.dad.state.vt.us/lp/New APS Pages/report-ingform.htm Vermont Department of Aging & Independent Living http://www.dad.state.vt.us/lp/
Virginia	1-888-83-ADULT or 1-888-832-3858 Richmond Area: 804-371-0896 Virginia Adult Protective Services http://www.dss.virginia.gov/family/aps.html	1-888-83-ADULT or 1-888-832-3858 Richmond Area: 804-371-0896
Washington	1-866-EndHarm or 1-866-363-4276 Washington Aging and Disability Services Admin-istration http://www.aasa.dshs.wa.gov/topics/abuse/ Adult Protective Services (APS) Regional Reporting Numbers http://www.aasa.dshs.wa.gov/library/publications/htmlversions/abuse.htm	1-800-562-6078

Report Elder Abuse		
West Virginia	1-800-352-6513 West Virginia Adult Protective Services http://www.wvdhhr.org/bcf/children_adult/aps/report.asp	1-800-352-6513
Wisconsin	608-266-2536 E-mail: StopAbuse@dhfs.state.wi.us Wisconsin Department of Health and Human Services http://dhfs.wisconsin.gov/aging/elderabuse/index.htm Wisconsin County Elder Abuse Agencies & Help Lines http://dhfs.wisconsin.gov/aging/elderabuse/agencies.htm	1-800-815-0015 (Toll free in Wisconsin) Outside of Wisconsin: 608-246-7013 Wisconsin Long Term Care Ombudsman http://dhfs.wisconsin.gov/aging/BOALTC/LTCOMBUD.HTM
Wyoming	1-800-457-3659 (Toll free in Wyoming) Outside of Wyoming: 307-777-6137 Wyoming Adult Protective Services http://dfsweb.state.wy.us/aps.htm Wyoming County Family/Adult Protective Services Agencies http://dfsweb.state.wy.us/protectivesvc/programs/aps/FieldOffices.htm	307-777-6137 or 307-777-7123 Wyoming Long Term Care Ombudsman http://www.wyomingseniors.com/ombudsman.htm

(Taken from Nccafv.org hotline)

Thank You

---

*T*hank you for using this resource to enhance your program or your loved one's life. To contact us personally, go to www.SeniorActivitiesForLifeEnrichment. com to ask questions, set up staff trainings, seminars or consultations.

May you and your loved ones celebrate the golden years with grace and dignity.

Terri L. Glimcher

Tammy J. Mackey